AF602077

ADDICTION TREATMENT OUTCOMES

Approved by:

Rene Drumm, Ph.D. MSW, Thesis
Adviser, Associate Dean, College of Health

Tim Rehner, Ph.D.,
Professor of Social Work Director School of
Social Work Chair, Council of Chairs

Ellen Weinauer, Ph.D., Dean
Honors College

The University of Southern Mississippi

ADDICTION TREATMENT OUTCOMES

All Roads lead to CHRIST

SIDNEY H. SMITH III

Addiction Treatment Outcomes

A Thesis Submitted to the Honors College of The University of Southern Mississippi in Partial Fulfillment of the Requirement for the Degree of Bachelor of Social Work in the School of Social Work

May 2018

Table of Contents

Abstract

This study examines how religiosity, specifically, church attendance, prior to admission into an addictions treatment facility (Teen Challenge) is related to the treatment outcomes of completing the program and the participants' length of stay in treatment. Additionally, the study investigates how other factors such as marital status, ethnicity, alcohol and drug use, and level of education may be related to treatment outcomes. Using archival data of 388 enrollees in a Teen Challenge program in southern United States, the results show that religiosity prior to treatment admission is significantly related to program completion. However, the second outcome variable, length of time in treatment was not significantly related to religiosity. The findings also reveal that education was positively related to length of treatment, but not program completion. While more study is needed to understand the relationship between religiosity and addiction program completion, this study confirms a positive relationship between church attendance prior to treatment and program completion.

Dedication

My son Jordan, Judy, Mom, Officer Steven Gill, Pastor Wilson, David Dilmore, Aaron Bratton, Chief Leonard Papania, Church of the Good Shepard, Rev. Leanne Burris, Campground Baptist, USM School of Social Work Faculty, 2018 BSW cohort, and Teen Challenge: Thank you for your unconditional love, infinite encouragement, and your ability to see me with God's eyes. All of you were purposely sent by God to invest in my life and the lives of others. Thank You!

Acknowledgements

I would like to thank my thesis advisor, Dr. Rene Drumm, for her patience in mentoring me. This work would not have been possible had it not been for her gentle, yet no non-sense spirit and tolerance of my inabilities and lack of knowledge where research is concerned. You are my mentor and I am forever grateful to you. Thank You!

To my wife Judy, there are no words that can express how truly grateful I am to have you as my wife. Proverbs 18:22

CHAPTER ONE

Introduction Problem Statement

Addiction in the United States is one of the largest national epidemics that plague our country. According to the National Survey on Drug Use and Health, an estimated 24.6 million individuals aged 12 or older were current illicit drug users in 2013 (National Survey on Drug Use and Health, 2014). The social problem of drug and alcohol abuse has resulted in twenty-two million addicts seeking treatment for their addictions (National Survey on Drug Use and Health, 2014).

Addiction brings high cost to society in terms of increased crime, family problems, economic woes and even death (Fischer, 2005). To address this problem, more than 14,500 specialized drug and alcohol treatment facilities operate nation-wide (NIDA, 2012). With 22 million people per year seeking help and relief from addiction through treatment centers in the United States, more research is needed to understand what factors contribute to positive treatment outcomes (NIDA, 2012).

CHAPTER TWO

Literature Review

Addiction Risk and Protective Factors

One way researchers and practitioners fight against the drug addiction epidemic is by developing a clearer understanding of the risk and protective factors that drive or repel addiction. Risk and protective factors operate across individual, family, community, and societal systems.

Some known factors that increase the risk of drug and alcohol addiction include early aggressive behavior, lack of parental supervision, peer substance abuse, drug availability, and poverty (NIDA, 2003). In addition, adolescents are at greater risk of addiction when their home environment is chaotic, their parents have a mental illness or abuse substances, they fail in school, or hold the belief that those around them approve of drug-using behaviors (NIDA, 2002). Research also demonstrates that there is an increased risk for hard drug abuse among adolescents who have been assaulted sexually, witnessed violence, and exposed to addiction via family members (Kilpatrick, Acierno, Saunders, Resnick, Best, & Schnurr, 2000).

Conversely, young people are more protected from drug and alcohol addiction when their family bonds are secure, their parents monitor their activities and enforce clear rules for appropriate behavior (NIDA, 2002). Further, when adolescents experience success in school and have ties to social institutions such as religious and civic organizations, they are better equipped to avoid drug addiction (NIDA, 2002).

As mentioned above, one factor that has a protective effect against drug use is religiosity/spirituality. Research indicates that communities of faith and religious institutions are important points of access in intervention, prevention, and reduction of drug use, HIV risk, and violence. A study by Drumm, McBride, Allen, and Baltzar, (2001), done with more than 1,200 participants, suggests that religious participation is related to abstinence, less drug use, and less risky behavior. Research data from this study suggests that even among addicts who are not in treatment, religious involvement serves as a protective factor.

Results demonstrated that street drug users who attended religious services reduced their drug use, decreased risky HIV behaviors, and engaged in less violent activities than users who did not attend services. Even though these studies, and others, indicate a protective effect of spirituality/religiosity on addiction, more in-depth examination of religion as a protective factor for drug use is warranted to understand how religion and spirituality might be used to enhance addiction treatment.

Addiction Treatment

Addiction treatment occurs in many forms such as short- and long-term residential treatment, outpatient treatment, individual and group counseling, and court-mandated treatment (NIDA, 2012). The two treatment approaches within these settings demonstrating the greatest record of success and having the broadest evidence-base include behavioral therapies and pharmacotherapy (NIDA, 2012). Pharmacotherapies consist of methadone, buprenorphine, and naltrexone. Behavior therapies include cognitive-behavior therapy, contingency management interventions, motivational enhancement therapy, and 12-step facilitation therapy (NIDA, 2012).

Spirituality and Addiction Treatment

Addiction treatment approaches such as those outlined above generally occur in one of two types of venues: secular and faith-based. Research on treatment settings documents that both types of venues may include religious activities which are either mandatory or voluntary depending on the setting (Davis, 2014). In a study examining 55 faith-based and secular programs, Davis (2014) found major differences in secular and faith-based addiction treatment program interventions with regard to incorporating spiritual or religious activities. Most faith-based addiction treatment programs mandate participation in religious practices; whereas, secular addiction treatment programs allow religious practices and consider them voluntary.

Whether treatment occurred in faith-based or secular settings, research on individuals engaged in or having completed addictions treatment report perceptions of the importance of incorporating spirituality as an enhancement to their treatment success (Hodge, 2014; Timmons, 2012; Allen, 2015; Blakey, 2016). In addition to anecdotal evidence about how the incorporation of spirituality enhances treatment outcomes, research suggests positive correlations between spirituality/religiosity, treatment retention, and enhanced abstinence (Wolf-Branigin, 2008; Chu, 2012; Heinz, 2007; Petry, 2008). Two of these studies (Heinz, 2007; Petry, 2008) evaluated religious/spirituality participation measuring drug screens and suggests enhanced treatment retention rates and better outcomes with drug use. Along the same line of research, Chu (2012) and Wolf-Branigin (2008) examined treatment completion affected by involvement and participation in spiritual activities and religious conversion and found differences between successful completions and non-completion. Religious conversion during treatment suggests significant enhanced completion rates to non–converts' treatment completion.

In contrast, a national study of more than 10,000 clients enrolled in 70 different treatment facilities showed mixed findings in terms of an individual's level of religiosity and retention in treatment and commitment to treatment (Shields, Broome, Delany, Fletcher, & Flynn, 2007). The findings revealed no significant relationship between retention rates and religiosity. However, researchers found a weak to moderate bivariate relationship indicating that participants with higher levels of religiosity have higher levels of commitment.

Similarly, another study demonstrated no significant differences in treatment outcomes between faith-based and secular treatment programs (Miller, 2008). The data collected in this study did not support the hypothesis that spiritual intervention positively impacted treatment outcomes. In fact, no significant impact of the spiritual intervention on substance use outcomes was found.

One explanation for the non-significant findings may reside with the dropout rates of the participants. The interventions that featured spiritual enrichment may have failed to show any benefit due to only 3-5 sessions being completed instead of the targeted 12 sessions.

Another reason may have been associated with the length of the program. With participants, just days out of detoxification and several life issues and other crises on their hands, recovery and self-actualization would be difficult to detect.

Teen Challenge

Teen Challenge is a well-known addiction treatment institution founded by David Wilkerson in 1958. It is a Christ-centered, faith-based, residential program providing solutions for those struggling with life controlling problems, such as drug and alcohol addiction (Global Teen Challenge, 2015). There are more than 1,100 Teen Challenge facilities in 118 countries, with more than 250 located in the United States. All of these facilities must be accredited and follow set policy and procedures (Teen Challenge International of Wisconsin, 2017).

Teen Challenge provides a 14-month residential program for adults who are 18 and older. Both men and women are served, but in separate facilities. The program has both a structured work program as well as an academic curriculum, with classroom instruction, Bible study, journaling, memorization of Scripture, and intensive writing assignments centered on 49- character qualities. Spirituality/religiosity is not required for admission to the Teen Challenge program. Not all clients are admitted to Teen Challenge voluntarily. Some are court ordered as an alternative to prison. Religious conversion is not a requirement for successful completion and graduation from the program.

The program is divided into two phases. The first phase can take six months or longer to complete, depending on the client, and includes a curriculum teaching accountability through a series of 14 books. The second phase consists of structured group sessions and counseling, with completion taking a minimum of eight months. The structured work program consists of vocational training in areas such as: welding, carpentry, operating machines, painting, car repair and detailing, and food preparation, as well as in more general areas, such as: team building, fund raising, management, customer service and computers (Teen Challenge International Wisconsin, 2017).

A study focusing on one Teen Challenge program, found that four elements of treatment contributed to recovery from substance abuse. The four key components were program structure, relationships with others, experiences of God, and individual initiative to make changes. Implementation of these components allowed the clients to experience a freedom from self and to find significance in putting others and the community first.

Freedom from self involves looking to the needs of others and putting personal needs aside. Through these four elements, the clients had changed views on life and their role in it. New values were assumed, and ways were found to put those values into action.

Those actions invariably centered on helping others and contributing to the community, which were not a high priority before Teen Challenge. Ultimately, by translating their new values into actions the clients found, and are still finding, a worthy life purpose (Allen, 2015).

In spite of these promising findings regarding the importance of spirituality on positive treatment outcomes, no studies on Teen Challenge programs have examined this relationship quantitatively. To address the question of how treatment outcomes may be related to clients' spiritual/religious practices, this study investigates the relationship between clients' religious/spiritual background and enhanced treatment retention and successful completion of treatment.

CHAPTER THREE

Methods

Participants and Data Collection

Archival data were collected from a regional Teen Challenge treatment facility in the Southern United States. Data were gathered from approximately 388 Teen Challenge client intake application records and corresponding discharge summaries. The initial intake applications are forms completed by the prospective clients, providing specific personal information and various questions about aspects of their current lives and history.

The corresponding discharge summaries are compiled by Teen Challenge staff once the clients have either completed the residential program successfully and graduated or have dropped out of the program. From the information provided on the forms, variables were coded and quantified, and the variables included: age, entry date, marital status (single, married, divorced), alcohol use (as a primary drug), drug use (How many other drugs used as primary), religiosity (Do you believe in God; Have you committed your life to God; Do you attend church on a regular basis), length of days in treatment, discharge status (discharged voluntarily or involuntarily), education (no high school diploma, high school diploma, more than high school), and program completion (graduated or discharged from the program).

Measures

This study examines successful addiction treatment and its association with religiosity at treatment intake. The analysis uses two measures of successful treatment:

(1) length of stay in treatment (retention rate), and (2) treatment outcomes (successful completion). The discharge summaries for treatment outcome note "graduated" for successful completion. Other options include, "voluntary" or "involuntary discharge" which indicate unsuccessful

treatment outcomes. From these variables, treatment outcomes were compartmentalized into two categories.

Length of stay in treatment was measured by the number of days a client stayed in treatment. Log transformation measure was used with the variable length of days to compensate the effects of data skewedness. Successful completion of treatment (graduated) was coded and quantified with yes (= 1), and unsuccessful treatment completion with no (= 0).

The independent variables included religiosity, drug and alcohol use, education, and marital status. The analysis used three different items to measure religiosity. The first question, "Do you believe in God?", was coded yes (=1), or no (=0). The second question, "Have you committed your life to God?" was coded yes (=1), or no (=0). The third question is, "Are you attending church?", and it was coded yes (=1), or no (=0).

Alcohol and drug use variables included: "Is alcohol a primary drug?" coded yes (=1), or no (=0). "Is heroin, powder cocaine, meth, barbiturates, prescription pills, marijuana, spice, opioids, or crack used on a regular basis?", and was coded yes (=1), or no (=0).

Educational levels were coded as follows: 0 represented no high school diploma, the number 1 represented a high school graduate, and the number 2 represented more education than high school. Marital status was coded in 3 categories: single (=1), married (=2), and divorced, widowed, or separated (=3).

Analysis

After quantifying and coding the data from the archived records, it was inputted into the Statistical Package for Social Sciences (SPSS). The three analytical procedures used to determine outcomes included chi-square, t-test, and analysis of variance.

A chi-square test was conducted to examine the relationship between church attendance and treatment outcomes (graduation, successful treatment, not graduating). The test focused on whether clients' religious involvement prior to treatment was significantly associated with their treatment outcomes. The same procedure was used with the other independent variables measured.

Secondly, a t-test was conducted to determine the relationship between length of days in treatment and church attendance. Lastly, an analysis of variance (ANOVA) was conducted to examine the relationship between education and length of days. In the results that follow, only the significant variables are reported.

CHAPTER FOUR

Results

Study Population

The sample included 388 archived data files. The demographics retrieved from the files reveals that 100% of the residents were male, primarily Caucasian, primarily single, and had a wide distribution of ages that range from the oldest client being 63- years-old, and the youngest client was 18-years-old. In terms of marital status, the majority of participants were single (71.3%), with nearly equal numbers being married (20.6%) and divorced (19.5%). Participants in treatment with no high school diploma numbered 34.7%, and participants with a high school diploma numbered 36.0%. The group with more than high school education was 29.1%.

Table 1. Demographics

Demographics	Type	Percent
Sex	Male	100%
Ethnicity	African American	10.1%
	Caucasian	88.1%
	Hispanic	1.9%
Marital Status	Married	20.6%
	Separated or Divorced	19.5%
	Single	71.3%
Education	Less than HS	34.7%
	High school	36.0%
	Some college	29.1%
Alcohol	Addiction	67.6%
	No Addiction	32.4%
Primary Drugs Use	1 drug	17%
	2 drugs	20.7%
	3 drugs	15.1%
	4 drugs	14.9%
	5 drugs	11.9%
	6 drugs	7.2%
	7 drugs	2.9%

	8 drugs	1.1%
	9 drugs	1.1%
	10 drugs	.5%
Religiosity - Do you believe in God?	Yes	95.2%
	No	4.8%
Spiritual activities	Regular involvement	32.9%
	No involvement	66.7%
Have you committed life to God?	Yes	76.4%
	No	23.6%
Graduation	Dropped out	83.5%
	Completed program	16.5%

Sample n=388

Number of days clients stayed in treatment varied for each individual. Some clients left treatment within the first few hours, others stayed longer than 14 months. The number of days in treatment ranged from one day up to 1,036 days for all 388 sampled clients.

Church Attendance and its Association with Treatment Outcomes

This study investigates the question, "Is church attendance at addiction treatment intake associated with positive treatment outcomes?" The findings which follow offer insights into this question as well the only other variable that was significantly related to positive treatment outcome—education.

Out of the 324 clients that dropped out of treatment, 33% of them attended church on a regular basis. As indicated in Table 2, there is higher percentage of clients regularly attending church that successfully completed treatment. Specifically, almost a quarter of the participants, (23%) successfully completed treatment who regularly attended church prior to treatment. Conversely, only 13% of the participants that reported no regular church attendance prior to admission, successfully completed the treatment. Chi-square analysis revealed this difference to be significant ($p < .011$). Thus, the association between church attendance prior to treatment and graduation rates was confirmed.

The second dependent variable focuses on the average length of days in treatment. Length of days in treatment is a continuous variable that was measured by the number of days the client stayed in treatment. Because the data is skewed, log transformation was performed on the variable. The differences between the average length of days in treatment for those who attended church prior to treatment admission and the participants who did not were measured with a t-test. The mean average length of days in treatment for participants who were attending church prior to entering treatment was 172.57 (SD = 203.59). The mean length of days the participants who were not attending church prior to treatment admission was 155.26 (SD= 185.48). Figure 1 shows t-test results of the differences between participants' t-test results (t = 1.74, p = .082). Thus, there were no statistically significant differences found between these two groups.

Figure 1. T-Test on Church Attendance and Length of Days in Treatment

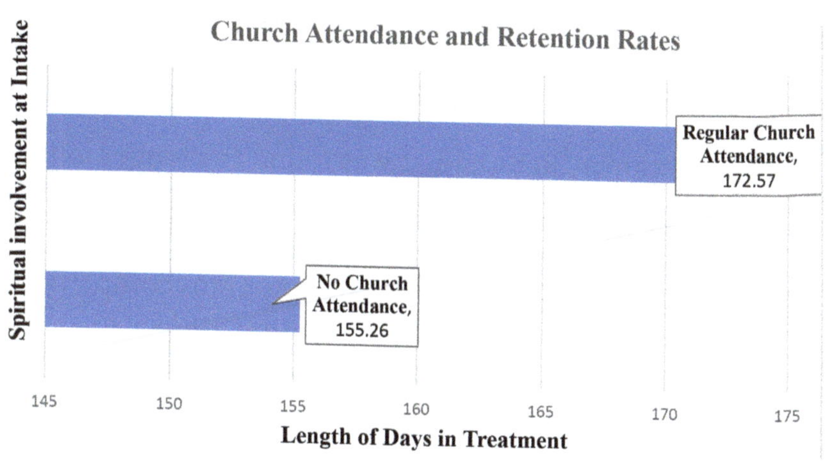

Education and its Association with Positive Treatment Outcomes

Education was examined to determine whether a significant relationship existed between length of days in treatment and education. An analysis of variance (ANOVA) was performed across the levels of education on the length of days (Figure 2).

Participants with no high school education stayed in treatment an average of 125.15 days (SD = 166.12). Participants with a high school diploma stayed in treatment an average of

172.20 (SD = 200.29), and the group of participants with more than a high school education stayed in treatment an average of 174.68 (SD = 202.87). These mean scores were significantly different, F (2,385) = 3.67, P = .026. The more education a client had, it was found the longer length of days in treatment they stayed. There were no significant relationships between education and program completion.

Figure 2. Education and Length of Stay in Treatment

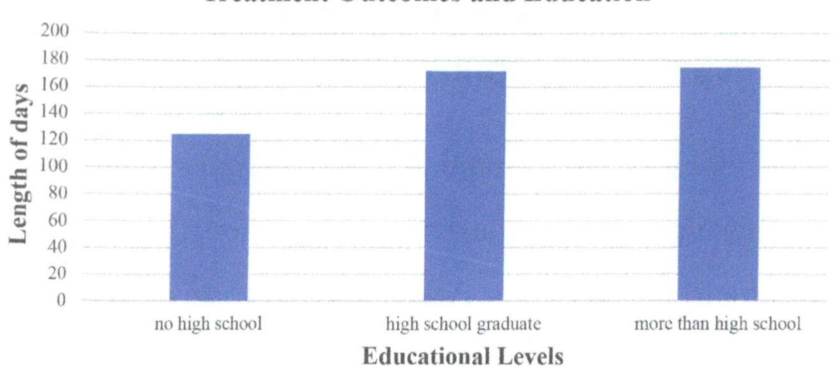

CHAPTER FIVE

Conclusions and Discussion

The findings of this study partially support the hypotheses. This study set out to find if a relationship existed between spirituality and successful treatment outcomes. It was found that regular church attendance prior to entering addiction treatment is associated with enhanced treatment outcomes through successfully completing the addiction program. Although regular church attendance prior to treatment intake was not significantly associated with length of days in treatment, the analysis showed the percentages in the expected direction and the chi-square approaching statistical significance.

Education was found to have a significant relationship with length of days in treatment. Specifically, clients with a high school diploma or a higher level of education stayed longer in treatment.

Current findings in this study have shown a relationship with the literature review on religious/spiritual involvement enhancing retention rates. The high drop-out rate among clients in this study is not unusual for drug and alcohol treatment facilities.

According to the research literature, high drop-out rates are normal when treatment is not mandatory by the courts, probation, and/or parole (Chu 2012).

The findings of this study still leave many unanswered questions. For example, "What is the definition of treatment outcomes or successful treatment completion?" Some researchers define treatment outcomes as no heavy drinking and reduced drug use (Strobbe, 2013; Matzger, 2005; Conner, 2009). This study measures treatment outcomes as successful when treatment is completed as well as length of days in treatment. Other studies in the literature review define treatment outcomes by a year of abstinence from drugs and alcohol, and the severity of the addiction (Piderman, 2008; Sterling, 2006; Ranes, 2017). There is no clear definition of what successful treatment looks like and no one way of measuring it. The instruments that are used to measure treatment outcomes vary from Alcoholics Anonymous Involvement, Alcohol Abstinence Efficacy Scale, and Drug Taking Confidence Questionnaires (Sterling,2006; Piderman, 2008).

While many questions remain unanswered, the data support that regular church attendance prior to treatment admission is associated with successfully completing the addiction program. More study is needed to further support this finding; however, it is a potentially useful avenue of future study.

References

Allen, L. M. (2015). Graduates' Perceptions on How "Teen Challenge Alberta" Influenced Them: A Grounded Theory Study (Ph.D.). University of Calgary (Canada), Canada. http://search.proquest.com.lynx.lib.usm.edu/docview/1754619734/abstract/D5697 D0B985049FDPQ/1

Blakey, J. M. (2016). The role of spirituality in helping African American women with histories of trauma and substance abuse heal and recover. *Social Work & Christianity*, 43(1), 40–59.

Chu, D. C., Sung, H.-E., & Hsiao, G. Y. (2012). Religious conversion and treatment outcome: An examination of clients in a faith-based residential substance treatment program. *Journal of Drug Issues*, 42(2), 197–209.

Davis, M. T. (2014). Religious and non-religious components in substance abuse treatment: A comparative analysis of faith-based and secular interventions. *Journal of Social Work*, *14*(3), 243–259. https://doi.org/10.1177/1468017313476589

Drumm, Rene, D., McBride, Duane C., Allen, Karen, & Baltzar, Alina. (2001). Protective effects. *Social Work*, *13*(3), 83–93.

Fischer, B. (2005). Illicit opioid use in Canada: Comparing social, health, and drug use characteristics of untreated users in five cities (OPICAN Study). *Journal of Urban Health: Bulletin of the New York Academy of Medicine*, 82(2), 250–266. https://doi.org/10.1093/jurban/jti049

Global Teen Challenge. (2015). Our story. Retrieved May 9, 2017, from http://globaltc.org/our-story/

Heinz, A., Epstein, D. H., & Preston, K. L. (2007). Spiritual/Religious Experiences and In-Treatment Outcome in an Inner-City Program for Heroin and Cocaine Dependence. *Journal of Psychoactive Drugs*, 39(1), 41–49.

Hodge, D. R., & Lietz, C. A. (2014). Using Spiritually Modified Cognitive--Behavioral Therapy in Substance Dependence Treatment: Therapists' and Clients' Perceptions of the Presumed Benefits and Limitations. *Health & Social Work*, 39(4), 200. https://doi.org/10.1093/hsw/hlu022

Kilpatrick, D. G., Acierno, R., Saunders, B., Resnick, H. S., Best, C. L., & Schnurr, P. P. (2000). Risk factors for adolescent substance abuse and dependence: Data from a national sample. *Journal Of Consulting And Clinical Psychology*, *68*(1), 19-30. doi:10.1037/0022-006X.68.1.19

Matzger, H., Kaskutas, L. A., & Weisner, C., (2005). Reasons for drinking less and their relationship to sustained remission from problem drinking.

Society for the Study of Addiction, 100, 1637-1646. doi: 10.1111/j/1360-0443.2005.01203.x

Miller, W. R., Forcehimes, A., O'Leary, M. J., & Lanoue, M. D. (2008). Spiritual direction in addiction treatment: Two clinical trials. *Journal of Substance Abuse Treatment*, 35(4), 434–442. https://doi.org/10.1016/j.jsat.2008.02.004

National Institute on Drug Abuse (March 2011). Treatment statistics. Retrieved May 9, 2017, from https://www.drugabuse.gov/publications/drugfacts/treatment-statistics

National Survey on Drug Use and Health. (2014, September 4). The NSDUH report: Substance use and mental health estimates from the 2013 national survey on drug use and health: Overview of findings. Retrieved April 19, 2017, from http://archive.samhsa.gov/data/2k14/NSDUH200/sr200-findings-overview- 2014.htm

National Institute on Drug Abuse. (2012). Drug addiction treatment in the United States.

Retrieved April 28, 2017, from https://www.drugabuse.gov/publications/principles-drug-addiction-treatment- research-based-guide-third-edition/drug-addiction-treatment-in-united-states

National Institute on Drug Abuse. (2002). https://archives.drugabuse.gov/NIDA_Notes/NNVol16N6/Risk.html

National Institute on Drug Abuse. (2003). What are risk factors. https://www.drugabuse. gov/publications/preventing-drug-abuse-among-children-adolescents/chapter-1- risk-factors-protective-factors/what-are-risk-factors

Petry, N. M., Lewis, M. W., & Østvik-White, E. M. (2008). Participation in Religious Activities During Contingency Management Interventions Is Associated with Substance Use Treatment Outcomes. *American Journal on Addictions*, *17*(5), 408–413. https://doi.org/10.1080/10550490802268512

Piderman, K. M., Schneekloth, T, D., Pankratz, V, S., Stevens, S. R., & Altchuler, S. I. (2008).

Spirituality during alcoholism treatment and continuous abstinence for one year. *International Journal of Psychiatry in Medicine, 38* (4), 391- 406.doi:10.2190/PM.38.4.a

Piedmont, R. (2004). Spiritual transcendence as a predictor of psychosocial outcome from an outpatient substance abuse program. *Psychology of Addictive Behaviors 18* (3), 213-222.doi:10.1037/0893-164X.18.3.213

Ranes, B. (2017). The role of spirituality n treatment outcomes following a residential 12- Step program. *Alcoholism Treatment Quarterly, 35* (1), 16-33. doi: 10.1080/07347324.2016.1257275

Shields, J. J., Broome, K. M., Delany, P. J., Fletcher, B. W., & Flynn, P. M. (2007).

Religion and substance abuse treatment: Individual and program effects. *Journal for the Scientific Study of Religion*, 46(3), 355–371. https://doi.org/10.1111/j.1468-5906.2007.00363.x

Sterling, R. C., Weistein, S., Hill, P., Gottheil, E., Gordon, S. M., Shorie, K., (2006).

Levels of spirituality and treatment outcome: A preliminary examination. *Journal of Studies on Alcohol, 67* (4) 600-606.

Strobbe, S., Cranford, J. A., Wojnar, M., & Brower, K. J. (2013). Spiritual awakening predicts improved drinking outcomes in a Polish treatment sample. *Journal of Addictions Nursing, 24* (4), 209-216. doi:10.1097/JAN.0000000000000002

Teen Challenge International of Wisconsin. (2017). National Institute on Drug Abuse report Retrieved May 7, 2017, from http://www.teenchallengeonline.com/about- us/how-successful-is-teen-challenge/national-institute-on-drug-abuse-report/

Timmons, S. M. (2012). A Christian faith-based recovery theory: Understanding God as sponsor. *Journal of Religion and Health*, 51(4), 1152–1164. https://doi.org/10.1007/s10943-010-9422-z

Wolf - Branigin, M., & Duke, J. (2008). Spiritual involvement as a predictor to completing a Salvation Army substance abuse treatment program. *Research on Social Work Practice*, 17(2), 239–245. https://doi.org/10.1177/1049731506294373

Appendix IRB Letter

INSTITUTIONAL REVIEW BOARD
118 College Drive #5147 | Hattiesburg, MS 39406-0001
Phone: 601.266.5997 | Fax: 601.266.4377 | www.usm.edu/research/institutional.review.board

NOTICE OF COMMITTEE ACTION

The project has been reviewed by The University of Southern Mississippi Institutional Review Board in accordance with Federal Drug Administration regulations (21 CFR 26, 111), Department of Health and Human Services (45 CFR Part 46), and university guidelines to ensure adherence to the following criteria:

- The risks to subjects are minimized.
- The risks to subjects are reasonable in relation to the anticipated benefits.
- The selection of subjects is equitable.
- Informed consent is adequate and appropriately documented.
- Where appropriate, the research plan makes adequate provisions for monitoring the data collected to ensure the safety of the subjects.
- Where appropriate, there are adequate provisions to protect the privacy of subjects and to maintain the confidentiality of all data.
- Appropriate additional safeguards have been included to protect vulnerable subjects.
- Any unanticipated, serious, or continuing problems encountered regarding risks to subjects must be reported immediately, but not later than 10 days following the event. This should be reported to the IRB Office via the "Adverse Effect Report Form".
- If approved, the maximum period of approval is limited to twelve months.
  Projects that exceed this period must submit an application for renewal or continuation.

PROTOCOL NUMBER: 17120707
PROJECT TITLE: Spirituality/Religiosity Addiction Treatment Outcomes. What is the Relationship?
PROJECT TYPE: Honor's Thesis Project
RESEARCHER(S): Sidney H. Smith III
COLLEGE/DIVISION: College of Health
DEPARTMENT: Social Work
FUNDING AGENCY/SPONSOR: N/A
IRB COMMITTEE ACTION: Expedited Review Approval
PERIOD OF APPROVAL: 12/07/2017 to 12/06/2018
Lawrence A. Hosman, Ph.D.
Institutional Review Board

www.ingramcontent.com/pod-product-compliance
Ingram Content Group UK Ltd.
Pitfield, Milton Keynes, MK11 3LW, UK
UKHW020140300726
14059UKWH00007B/3